OPERATIONS

عملية Operación Opération Operation 行动 Операция

MOEZ SURANI

BookThug 2016

Canada Council Conseil des Arts  ONTARIO ARTS COUNCIL
for the Arts du Canada CONSEIL DES ARTS DE L'ONTARIO
an Ontario government agency
un organisme du gouvernement de l'Ontario

Funded by the Financé par le | **Canadä**
Government gouvernement
of Canada du Canada

The production of this book was made possible through the
generous assistance of the Canada Council for the Arts and the
Ontario Arts Council. BookThug also acknowledges the support of
the Government of Canada through the Canada Book Fund and the
Government of Ontario through the Ontario Book Publishing Tax
Credit and the Ontario Book Fund.

LIBRARY AND ARCHIVES CANADA
CATALOGUING IN PUBLICATION

Surani, Moez, 1979-, author
    Ḥamlah, operación, opération, operation, xing dong,
operatsīiā / Moez Surani. — First edition.

Poem.
Parts of the title romanized.
Issued in print and electronic formats.
ISBN 978-1-77166-268-0 (PAPERBACK)
ISBN 978-1-77166-269-7 (HTML)
ISBN 978-1-77166-270-3 (PDF)
ISBN 978-1-77166-271-0 (KINDLE)

    I. Title. II. Title: Operation.

PS8637.U74.H34 2016   C811'.6   C2016-905014-9
                                          C2016-905015-7

PRINTED IN CANADA

INTRODUCTION

ONE

This is a poem of violence. It is a collection of the names of military operations conducted by member states of the United Nations (UN) from the UN's inception in October 1945, to the incorporation of the Responsibility to Protect (R2P) document in 2006. The title is the word "operation" in the six official languages of the UN: Arabic, Spanish, French, English, Chinese and Russian. The poem that follows is a globe-spanning inventory of the contemporary rhetoric of violence and aggression.

Representatives from fifty countries gathered in San Francisco in April 1945, and by the end of June an agreement was reached to create an international system unifying these countries. President Truman declared that this constituted "a solid structure upon which we can build a better world" and "a victory against war itself." In light of the events of the Second

World War and military activities since that time, his belief in the promise of that document now appears naïve. Most prophetic was his conclusion: "If we fail to use it we shall betray all those who have died so that we might meet here in freedom and safety to create it. If we seek to use it selfishly—for the advantage of any one nation or any small group of nations—we shall be equally guilty of that betrayal."

The UN's birth in 1945 is the opening frame of this poem. A second UN document, the Responsibility to Protect, sixty-one years later, is the closing frame. The R2P language emerged from UN Secretary General Kofi Annan's question to the public in 2000: "If humanitarian intervention is, indeed, an unacceptable assault on sovereignty, how should we respond to a Rwanda, to a Srebrenica—to gross and systematic violations of human rights that offend every precept of our common humanity?" Twelve people met in Ottawa to determine how to rightfully breach a country's sovereignty to prevent calamity. Their answer: a government has a responsibility to protect its citizens. When this responsibility is abdicated, the UN can rightfully intervene.

With this poem beginning at the outset of the UN and closing at the 2006 ratification of the R2P language, this framing embodies a movement in the poem itself, away from conflicts between countries and towards those within them.

TWO

During World War Two, Winston Churchill wrote a memo with directives for how to name British military operations:

I.   Operations in which large numbers of men may lose their lives ought not to be described by code words which imply a boastful or overconfident sentiment . . . or, conversely, which are calculated to invest the plan with an air of despondency. . . .

II.   They ought not to be names of a frivolous character. . . . They should not be ordinary words often used in other connections. . . Names of living people—Ministers and Commanders—should be avoided. . . . After all, the world is wide, and intelligent thought will readily supply an unlimited number of well-sounding names which do not suggest the character of the operation or disparage it in any way and do not enable some widow or mother to say that her son was killed in an operation called "Bunnyhug" or "Ballyhoo."

III.   Proper names are good in this field. The heroes of antiquity, figures from Greek and Roman mythology, the constellations and stars, famous racehorses, names of British and American war heroes, could be used, provided they fall within the rules above.

These rules are still observable today. Most of the names, even those American ones that were generated automatically but altered and approved by the Joint Chiefs of Staff, have dignity, an inspirational loft, a sense of worthiness and tend towards the heroic.

THREE

Who wrote this poem? Over the past four years, I've treated عملية *Operación Opération Operation* 行动 *Операция* as a piece on which 193 countries have inadvertently collaborated. But who, specifically, is responsible for draping *County Fair* over the menace of an operation in Vietnam? Or for *Grapple* being the sign under which nuclear weapons detonated high above the Pacific? Even thinking of this as a collaboration forsakes precision. Who are the authors—the committees or those at the top tiers of command—who selected these names and sent them down through their fighting ranks and out into the international media?

Despite my effort, this piece is simply a gesture towards the comprehensive poem that I've failed to fully excavate. When I began, I envisioned it encompassing all the names and for it to be so perfect that no matter the researcher— whether in Geneva, Toronto or Seoul—the resulting text would be identical. I had to concede that this isn't exhaustive; it would be different if it was done by another. One of the difficulties encountered in the composition process is that communist countries were harder to research than non-communist countries. This poem, then, has shadow entries, names of military operations nested between those cited that I failed to discover. The second complication is the number of judgment calls needed to determine whether an operation belonged on this list or not. What if it was a police operation and not a military one? Or if the source was not a government document, but a less official one— one that doesn't boast the same stature and veracity? The police operations, I omitted; operations derived from folk documents, I have included. So the entries *Hammer* (a 1987 Los Angeles Police Department operation targeting gang violence), *Trident* (a 1998 London Metropolitan Police operation targeting gun violence) or *Fire for Fire* (a 2001 Nigerian operation to counter armed robberies) are absent. But *Albacete* (a 1960 exercise in Spain) and *Ixil* (a Guatemalan operation targeting internal subversives) are present.

Following these parameters, I've also omitted operation names by non-governmental organizations that aren't signatories to the UN's charter. Because of this, the operation names of, for example, the Tamil Tigers do not fit within this text. So in this poem it could appear as though the Sri Lankan army, in *Thunder Strike*, *Fire Flame* and *Battle Cry*, was fighting ghosts.

FOUR

I love names. *Tulip. Beanbag. Butterfly. Flying Dagger.*
I love the second book of the *Iliad* where the text is
bloated with them: Abantes, Adrastus, Lycastos. Or
Parque de la Memoria in Buenos Aires that recognizes
the victims of fourteen years of Argentine state terror
and genocide. Nine thousand names are engraved on
those stones and another twenty-one thousand stones
remain deliberately blank. And Maya Lin's monument
in Washington that a friend and I discovered by
accident one night while following a path west from
the Washington Monument until we found ourselves
standing in front of something we didn't quite know:
a wall of names. We realized where we were, and what
we were standing amidst, as we read those names.

FIVE

I became interested in operation names in 2003. I was
an undergraduate, and as I followed the brinksmanship
between America and Iraq, I naively believed Baghdad
wouldn't be bombed. There wasn't enough proof; it
wasn't a persuasively just war. I assumed that martial
rhetoric was a way to leverage bargaining power. On
the night of March 19, I was studying for a mid-term
when a friend found me, and we ran with our things
to a campus bar and watched the bombing in the
eerily green night vision of the CNN broadcast. The

name of that military operation was *Infinite Justice*. My friend and I stared at the screens and wondered when it would possibly end.

We weren't alone in our apprehension at that name. There were so many others who reacted this way, in fact, that the name was changed to one more unambiguously noble: *Operation Iraqi Freedom*. A change like this, when a name doesn't play in the public in the way it is intended to, happens a few times in the poem. In spring 2005, when Robert Mugabe wanted Zimbabwean slums cleared out so the land could be used for another purpose, he named this domestic operation *Murambatsvina. Drive Out Rubbish*. When this name was made public and people objected, the name had to be changed to something more dignified so, it became *Restore Order*. On these occasions, I've included both: *Infinite Justice / Iraqi Freedom*. The backslash can be read as an equal sign; since the two names signify the same action, they are linguistically equivalent.

SIX

While researching the concept of heroism, I discovered that the word derives from the origins of the word "hour." Heroes are those who reconcile themselves to the proper minute of their deaths. Strictly speaking, then, heroism cannot be forced upon someone; it must arise from one's own volition. Many of the names herein invoke the heroic. But did all the people involved in these conflicts, whose names haunt the margins of this poem, find their proper hour? Does the Greek notion of the heroic suit them? Or is every invocation of the heroic evidence of the fantasies of governments?

SEVEN

This poem is also an index of stories. Each name is the residue of an action that's often hotly contested, because what's at stake is a country's sense of virtue or identity. Each entry, then, is a trial where judgment can be passed on the instigating country's moral authority.

EIGHT

While many names invoke or vilify an opponent, there's a subset in which the antagonist isn't another country but the earth itself: *Crossroads* (1946), an American nuclear test detonated near the Marshall Islands in the Pacific, or *Gerboise Bleue* (1960), a French nuclear detonation in Algeria, or *Tsar Bomba* (1961), which represented the planet's largest weapon, detonated by Russia in one of their northern archipelagos. This is large-scale violence done to a passive and stoic combatant: nature.

NINE

The cover of this book is from the Red Series by Brazilian artist Rosângela Rennó, made in 2000. This particular piece is "Untitled (hangman)." The source material for these images were photo albums collected from different countries and curated for photos of civilians dressed in military clothing. The colouring is her manipulation. Just as the gear and pose spread from the military into the civilian realm, in this poem militaries adopt a shared, often colloquial speaking register. *Gravy. Dragonfly. Wind.* These names aren't some alpha numeric argot for insiders, but a common and often pastoral vocabulary. The poem and Rennó's piece reveal the two realms, military and civilian, as inextricably linked; any semblance of separation is cosmetic.

TEN

Two images recur in naming military operations: dawn and cleanliness. *Morning Light, June Dawns, Before the Dawn, Red Dawn, Sunrise, New Dawn. Cleansing, Total Cleansing, Clean Up, Clean Corridor, Clean Sweep, Clean and Beautiful, Clean House.* Both expose a nation's dreams of purity and implicitly connect this aesthetic of purity to a ritual genocide: the purity of tomorrow, which the military operation promises, justifies the violence of tonight. The implication is that the military campaign will bring renewal and a clean slate: a dreamier country without tension, dirt, darkness or mess. These names animate this wish. If someone wanted to defy the rhetoric and disarm the persuasive tug of these oft-invoked names, what they would have to do is dream of and work towards nations that coveted impurity.

ELEVEN

What I've found is that no word is exempt from connoting violence. This poem makes "tulip" and "grasshopper" equal to "killer" and "bone breaker." No word is inherently innocent, beautiful or good.

Also preoccupying me as this poem lengthened was Walter Lippmann's explanation of how to measure the health of a democracy. He wrote that democratic health is related to the vitality of the media and the education of citizens. These three factors strengthen or decay together. It follows then that operation names that obfuscate their intentions depress the robustness of democracies. They conceal intention, delay understanding, and, in place of thoughtful engagement, appeal to emotions or valour. But if a citizen's personal values matched those of the military operations conducted by their country, an operation ought to be named with perfect candour. This lack of candour, and the propensity for euphemisms, exposes a chasm between personal and national values. The bits of language that follow document this gap.

TWELVE

Concepcion Picciotto was born in 1936 in Francisco Franco's Spain. She was nine years old in the year this poem begins. In 1960, she moved to New York, married, and adopted a young girl from Argentina. In 1981, with political buttons on her shirt proclaiming her pacifism, she began the action that gave her fame: a thirty-year peace vigil across from the White House, the longest political protest in American history. A collection of her signs and buttons include: "Read My Lips, No New Wars," "Live by the Bomb, Die by the Bomb," "No more troops!," "Ban All Nuclear Weapons or Have a Nice Doomsday," and "Silence is a War Crime." From her tarp-covered tent, she faced the stately neoclassicism of the White House. This morning as I write this, I see that she died, at eighty, just a few hundred feet away from the location of her protest. The *New York Times* obituary describes her as Nobel Peace Prize–winner Barack Obama's closest neighbour.

Moez Surani
February, 2016

عملية Operación Opération Operation 行动 Операция

And now, O Muses, dwellers in the mansions of Olympus, tell me—
for you are goddesses and are in all places so that you see all
things, while we know nothing but by report
—Homer, *Iliad*, Book Two

The Purposes of the United Nations are: To develop friendly relations
among nations based on respect for the principle of equal rights and
self-determination of peoples, and to take other appropriate measures
to strengthen universal peace
—United Nations, "Charter of the United
Nations" (1945), Ch. I, Art. I (2)

1945

Clobber
Haystack

1946

Archery
Asylum
Bille
Blizzard
Copyright
Goodwood
Homing Pigeon
Honeybee
Hunger III
Marriages
Olympic
Sandstone
Stork
Trademark
Wasp
Whisk
Surgeon
Epilogue
Freshman
Ribbon
Keynote
Puff

Sam
Wallop
Nipoff
Swallow
Heartbreak
Outward
Squeeze
Castanets
Kipper / Faggot
Davy Jones' Locker
Agatha
Crossroads
Tabarin
Shark
Keelhaul
Marriage
High Jump
Mudlark
Woodpecker
Oasis
Odeon
Retail
Octopus
Pedestal

1947

Asbtract / Bad Sachsa / Oberjoch
Blackcurrant

Curfew
Folium
Happy Return
Hunger IV
Inkpot
Mackerel
Old Lace
Sandfly
Sparkler
Stockpile
Traffic
Westward Ho
Source
Cantonment
Crossline
Polly
Roundabout
Eastwind
Fleacomb
Posterity
Valuable
Papillon [Butterfly]
Wisła [Vistula]
Diagram
Product
Tiger
Terminus
Bluecoat
Grand National

Totalize
Léa
Windmill
Rollup
Ceinture [Belt]
Veritable

1948

Bystander
Caravan
Double Quick
Greenford
Harness
Journey's End
Pickle
Pinstripe
Planet
Second Slip
Smoke
Snooker
November
Seahawk
Stress
Itzuv [Stabilization]
Hashmed [Destroy]
נחשון [Nachshon]
Dawn
Sandstone

Harel [Mountain of God]

ביעור חמץ [Passover Cleaning]

יבוסי [Yevusi]

Misparayim [Scissors]

חמץ [Leaven]

יפתח [Opens]

Seanuts

מטאטא [Broom]

Maccabi

ברק [Lightning]

Gideon

Kilshon [Pitchfork]

בן עמי [Ben-Ami]

שפיפון [Rattler]

Tinok [Baby]

Gulab [Rose]

Namel [Port]

Bin Nun Alef / Nun's Son

Erez [Cedar]

פלשת [Philistia]

Bin Nun Bet

Paladin

Yitzhak [Isaac]

Yoram

Balak

Bloodstone

Firedog

Knicker

Plainfare

Vittles

Plainfire

Coronis

Anti-Farouk / An-Far

Kedem

דקל [Palm Tree]

Brosh [Cypress]

דני [Danny]

מות לפולש [Death to Invader]

שוטר [Policeman]

מבצע גי"ס [Gayis]

Little Vittles

מבצע גי"ס [Gayis II]

Double Cross

Eraze / Duck/ Bison

Way to the Negev

אבק [Dust]

Polo

Pelican

Velvetta / Alabama

Yoav [Ten Plagues]

ההר [Mountain]

Hiram

Easy

שמונה [Eight]

לוט [Lot]

אסף [Assaf]

Geranium

Velvetta II / Alabama II

Kraai [Crow]

Horev

התחלה [Beginning]

1949

Artisan

Cowbane

House Party

Link

Magnet

Powerstrike

Rusty

Scrum Half

Silver

Subsmash

Exodus

Whizzbang

Turnover

עובדה [Fact]

Priboi [Coastal Surf]

Magic Carpet / On Wings of Eagles /
    Messiah's Coming

Pyrsos [Torch]

Union

Branmash

Refine

1950

Carat

House Party II

Kidney

Weary

Farmstead

Vast

Musgrave

Renault

Off Load

Chow Chow

Immediate

Pokpoong [Storm]

Order 8-50

Salamander

Flush-Out

Bout One

인천 상륙 [Blue Hearts]

Hawk

Nannie Able

Nannie Baker

Rebuild

Nannie Charles

Shoe String

Lee

Manchu

Epicure

Trudy Jackson

Booklift
Chromite
Common Knowledge
Aviary
Order 9-50
Chiến dịch Biên giới [Sovereign Borders]
Comeback
Tailboard
Paper / Greeting October
Defrost
Rat Killer
Blossom
Pink
Kiddie Car
Turnaround
Long-Johns
Snap
Christmas Kidlift
Kiddie Car Lift
Little Orphan Annie
Santa Claus
Sleigh Ride
Relax

1951

Accent
Basket
Chivalrous

French Pastry
Mikado
Mockingbird
Rockaway
Rodeo Flail
Stole
Tannenberg
Lawn Mower
Leopard
Downpour
Moonbeam
Wolfhound
Thunderbolt
Ranger
Ascendant
Tack
Exploitation
Punch
Roundup
P
Killer
Rotate
Poster
Shining Moon
Wellsend
Ripper
Virginia 1
Hawk
Courageous

Tomahawk
Ripper Linkup
Rugged
Dauntless
Iron Triangle
Greenhouse
Fireball
Sea Dragon
Audacious
Haircut
Albany
Ashcan
Big Ben
Cigarette
Squeegee
Strangle
Ezra and Nehemiah
Mousetrap
Initiate
Chopper
Follow-up
Paper
Piledriver
Goose
Spitfire
Firefly
Maindy
Cat and Dog
Bonn / Wahner Heide

Doughnut
Farmer
Boar
Cave Dweller
Kickoff
Cow Puncher
Slam
Punchbowl
Dirk
Citadel
Claymore
Big Boy
Boomerang
Mustang II
Minden
Ohio Sloan
Windmill I
Clean Up I
Cudgel
Windmill II
Cleaver
Summit
Snatch
Blackbird
Pelican
Clean Up II
Snowball
Commando
Retribution

Touchdown
Hudson Harbour
Bumblebee
Nomad-Polar
Polecharge
Wedge
Bushbeater
Buster-Jangle
Pepperpot
Rabbit Hunt
House Burning I
House Burning II
Touchy
Tulipe / Tulip
Sundial
Switch
Counter Punch
Freeze Out
Skunk Hunt
Skyhook
Cheerful
Farewell
Helicopter

1952

Aberdeen
Admaston
Concubine

Eagle
Gondola
Joint
Mainbrace
Moonlight Sonata
Neutralize
Purvey
Rotor
Storm Trooper
Thrush
Tigress
Wolfpack
Arson
Canidus
Mustang III
Broken Reed
Yeshbum
Changie Changie
Derail
Highboy
Package
Junket
Chicken Stealer
Beechers Brook
Clam-Up
Decoy
Snare
Liverpool
Polecat

Amarante [Amaranth]

Get Well

Saturate

Avalanche

Native Son Dog

Roof Lifter

Alcatraz

Mustang IV

Mixmaster

Dew I

Sauterelle [Grasshopper]

Chopstick 6

Tumbler-Snapper

Scatter

Marlex I

Pronto

Mascot

Tropic

Clobber

Fishnet

Westminster

Chopstick 16

MiG

Ferret

Leapfrog

Spreadout

Dew II

Circus

Removal

Timber

Breakup

Muffler

Mule Train

Whoomph

Insomnia

Mustang V

Mustang VI

Strike

Ungeziefer [Vermin]

Butterfly

High Tide

Everready

Amazon

Pressure

Blaze

Firecracker

Homecoming / Big Stick

Pressure Pump

Distemper

Little Joe

Nostril

Panther

Buffalo

Ripple I

Hajji Baba

Eve

Round Trip

Get Ready

Fortune

Siciro

Silent Redline I

Plan Eightbind

Haylift I

Plan Blast

Hurricane

Mayu

Red Cow

Amber Liquid

Red Frog

Feint

Nebraska

Showdown

Wrangler

Jock Scott

Mustang VII

Mustang VIII

Lorraine

Ivy

Trojan

Greek II

Pimlico

Beat Up

Bretagne

Thanksgiving

Janus

War Dance

Fauna

Santa Claus
Christmas Drop
Jesse James
Spotlight

1953

Antiquary
Awkward
Border
Cauldron
Durbex
Gladio / Sheepskin
Hesperus
Hurdle
Redeployment
Tanker
Weldfast
Paralysis
Bimbo
Buckshot
Green Dragon
Smack
Rattle / Profit
Ripple v
Clambake
Doorstop
Boxer
Boxer II

Boxer III

Silent Redline V

Boxer IV

Dog

Haylift II

Charlie

Nicotine

Tennis

Barbula

Terry Blue

Item

Upshot-Knothole

Spring Thaw

Roundup / Bataan

Hurricane

Rabbit I

Moolah

Rainbow

Rabbit II

Adolphe

Fast Shuffle

Once Again

Little Switch

Left Hook

Supercharge

Shakedown

Skyhook

Beehive

Counter

No Doze

Skyway

Pandora

Pappy

Buttercup

Hirondelle [Swallow]

Camel

Camargue

Big Switch

Spyglass

Ajax

Boot

Kittens

Back Door

Top Hat

שושנה [Shoshana]

Mouette [Seagull]

Totem

Brochet [Pike]

Castor [Beaver]

1954

Bagpipes

Defiant

Elba Isle

Field Mouse

Hat Box 1953

Hot Box

Strategy

Tartan

Wedgewood

Kufire

Jade

Atlante

Quicksilver

Washtub

Haul Ass

Castle

Spitfire

Cravat

Rodeo

Anvil

Condor D (Desperado)

Longshot 2

Hardrock Baker

Success

Forget-Me-Not

History

Broom

Susannah

Glory

Passage to Freedom

Gold

Stopwatch

Monsoon

First Flute

Thunderbolt

Winkle

1955

Alpha
Debenture
Deepfreeze
Doubleshuffle
Dragon Return
Hermes
Negation
Nervine / Lurcher
Sanjak
Snowdrop
Suntan
Yated [Stake]
Zipper
Chui
Teapot
חץ שחור [Black Arrow]
Longshot 1
Gimlet
Wigwam
אלקיים [Elkayam]
יונתן [Jonathan]
Bonaparte
אגד [Egged]
הר געש [Volcano]
Deep Freeze
Gnat
עלי זית [Olive Leaves]

1956

African Tour

Circus II

Goldflake

Mileage

Purse-net

Rats

Sandcastle

Terrapin

Circus

Apollo

Flashlight

Redwing

Glimmer

Aquatone

Mosaic

Lucky Alphonse

Poker

Revise

גוליבר [Gulliver]

לולב [Lulav]

Buffalo

Alacrity

Samaria

Sparrowhawk

Вихрь [Whirlwind]

תרנגול [Rooster]

Kadesh [Holy]

Mousquetaire [Musketeer]
Omer
Steamroller
Machbesh [Press]
Telescope
Omelette
Harridan
Safe Haven

1957

Albert
Brotherhood
Deepfreeze III
Dementia
Double March
Grape
Jackpot
King Canute
Pillar-box
Thursday
Tims
Tripper
Unsparing
Mantelpiece
Grapple
Plumbbob
Hurricane
Antler

Deep Water
Grapple x
Large Area Coverage / LAC

1958

Cut Out
Deepfreeze IV
Dimension
Grapple Zulu
Lighthouse
Matchbox
Orion
Quick Flight
Repack
Turtle / Valiant
Unicorn
Vague I
Whippet
Linesman
Quickfire
Rabbits
Grapple Y
Newsreel
Hardtack I
Corse
Fast Ball
Verano [Summer]
Fire Hydrant

Fortitude
Blue Bat
Order
West Wind
Grapple Z
Black Magic
Argus I
Argus II
Argus III
Hardtack II

1959

Burnt Cork
Concord
Executor
Friendship
Grapple M
Ice
Mastodon
Repack II
Shuttlecock
Sputnik
Trousseau
Vague II
Vixen
Visage
Hotfoot / White Star
Jumelles [Binoculars]
Orpheus

1960

Bailiff
Longstop
Master
Medstead
Optimist / Heel
Rum Tub II
Seagull
Stowage
Stunsail
Victor Search
Trawl
חרגול [Grasshopper]
40
Rigmarole
Poden
Albacete
Sullivan
Trade Wind
Catechism
Pasukan Gerilya 100 [Guerilla Forces 100]
Pedro Pan [Peter Pan]

1961

Almond
Ayres
Cowboy
Deputy

Enclose

Gallop

Legacy

Longlook

Pandemic

Post Report

Precedent

Vixen B1

Clearwater

Silk Purse

Vulpine

34A

New Tape

Pluto (Pipe-Lines Under the Ocean)

Puma

Falcon

Zapata

Tight Squeeze

Frente Leste [Eastern Front]

Kingfisher

Vantage

Bouledogue [Bulldog]

Charrue Longue [Long Plow]

Sandy Beach

Rumpunch

Morthor

Pasukan Gerilya 200 [Guerilla Forces 200]

Nougat

Farm Gate

Paktong

Palaci

ויכי [Prepare]

Mattock

Mongoose

Unikat

वजिय [Victory]

Trikora

1962

Accolade

Alexus

Blayberry

Brigadoon / Dominic

Chaldee

Charterhouse

Dermot

Hope Not

Mandala [Theatre]

Ranch Hand / Trail Dust

Pasukan Gerilya 300 [Guerilla Forces 300]

Lam Son 719

סנונית [Swallow]

Sunrise

Dominic

32-59

Анадырь [Anadyr]

Storax

Sunbeam
Fishbowl
Damocles
Jayawijaya [Victory Over Colonialism]
Kama
Leghorn
Grand Slam
Manuel

1963

Ale
Ayres II
Dormer
Fortress
Guilder
Impala
Parrot
Sandy Beach II
Trader
冷藏 [Coldstore]
Flaxman
Roller Coaster
Bargold
מבצע יהלום [Diamond]
Switchback / Parasol
Blowdown
Halutz [Pioneer]
Niblick
Hard Surface

1964

Blue Thread

Crackerjack

Forefront

Montrose

Pampas

Pedal

Piano Solo / Alone

Pioneer

Sampan

Small Boy

Tumpas [Annihilation]

Tunley

Neptune

Brother Sam

Inspectorate

חד וחלק [Plain and Simple]

Gravy / Porcupine

Snowgoose

Lam Son 115

Tridente [Trident]

Leaping Lena

Yankee Team

Spring Meet

Claret

Whetstone

Triangle

CHASE (Cut Holes and Sink 'Em) 1

Le Loi 9

Pierce Arrow
Lien Lu 7
CHASE (Cut Holes and Sink 'Em) 2
Dragon Noire [Black Dragon]
Dragon Rouge [Red Dragon]
Dragon Blanc [White Dragon]
Barrel Roll

1965

Caper
Charlotte
Dominic
Ferret
Loyalist
Mizzen
Talcum Altair
Vigilant
Flaming Dart
Flaming Dart II
Footboy
Rolling Thunder
Plei Me
Market Time
Sherwood Forest
Steel Tiger
Power Pack
Mayflower
Article

Blockbuster

Faun Fare

Arc Light

17-65

CHASE (Cut Holes and Sink 'Em) 3

Flintlock

Song Song River

Truong Cong Pen

19-65

Lien Ket 4 [Link 4]

Blast Out

Marble Mountain

Sadar [Awareness]

Gibraltar

Thunderbolt

Frag Order 12-65

Quang Tin

Binh Dinh [Pacify]

Quang Nam (1965)

Midnight

Anvil

Starlite

Barracuda

Highland / Ramrod

Grand Slam

Phu Dung [Hibiscus]/ Project Shining Brass
/ Prairie Fire

Venture

Stomp

Dwarka / Somnath

Piranha

Cold Steel

Cactus

Cairns

24-65

CHASE (Cut Holes And Sink 'Em) 4

Good Friend I

High Tide

Dagger Thrust

Hard Rock

Dagger Thrust II

Sayonara

Red One

Blue Bonnet / Red Bayonet

Checkerboard

Dagger Thrust III

Good Friend II

Quick Draw

Frag Order 15-65

Hopscotch

Xray One

Spread Out

Iron Triangle

Cobra / Settlement

Concord

Shiny Bayonet

Black Lion

Happy Valley

Lonesome End
Checkmate
Flip Flop
Depth
Fly Low
Settlement
Bushmaster Bravo
Trail Boss
Trail Blazer
Triple Play
Hot Foot
Ranger 1
Silver Bayonet
Indian Scout
Amos
New One
Red Snapper
27-65
All the Way
Long Reach
Revenger
Indian Scout
90
Big Horn
Hercules
Drum Head
Triple Trouble
Lien Ket 10
Binder 1

Custer Flats
Cutlass
Dagger One
Viper I
Binder II
Copperhead
Black Ferret
Binder III
Binder IV
Hump
Lightning
Fierce Mustang
Blue Marlin
Hop Out
Road Runner
Bushmaster
Corn
Docket I
Blue Marlin II
Road Runner II
Apache Brave
Road Runner III
Silver Bayonet II
New Life 65
Road Runner IV
Song Ve 6
Turkey Shoot
Rabbit Hunt
Bushmaster II / Bloodhound

Dagger Thrust IV
Riviera
Big Drum
Choc Ice
Peter
Short Trek
Ox Trail
Dagger Thrust V
Tiger Hound
Charger Sweep
Give Up
Gladiator
Feline
Harvest Moon
Bushmaster III
Lien Ket 18 [Link 18]
Sweeping Mustang
Fish Hook
Quick Kick (1965)
Bear Trap
Frisk
Fish Hook II
Viper II
Clean House I
Smash I & II
Beaver
Frisk II
Fulton
Scalping Mustang

Game Warden
Clean House II
Jingle Bells
Blue Light / Holokai XII
Cherokee Trail
Little Sheba
Clean House III
Hoa Xuan Island
Cherokee Brave
Take Out
Rebel Rouser

1966

Brumby
Drum Major
Goatskin
Jefferson
Marauder / An Dan 564 [People's Peace]
Matador
Radsur
Rough Ride
Sailor Hat
Stag's Head
Hang Over
Long Lance
Quick Kick (1966)
War Bonnet
Crimp

Flying Tiger vi

Mallard

Quick Kick ii

Buckskin

Short Fuse

Matador ii

Quick Hop

Tyler

Big Lodge

Red Ball iv

Pioneer i

Van Buren

Retriever i

Kamehameha [The Very Lonely One]

Lightning Bug

Hot Tip

Masher / White Wing / Thang Phong ii

Pioneer ii

Quick Kick iii

Retriever ii

Double Eagle

Mallet

Red Ball v

Kamehameha ii [The Very Lonely One ii]

Bob Cat

Bobcat Tracker

Quick Kick iv

Taro Leaf

Roundhouse

White Wing
Taylor
Reconstruction
Road Runner VI
Taut Bow
Bald Eagle
Kamehameha III [The Very Lonely One III]
Rolling Stone
Entrée
Evansville
Breezeway
Paddy Bridge
Eagle's Claw
Belt Line
Double Eagle II
Harrison
Mastiff
Clean Sweep
Garfield
Kolchak I
Phoenix
New York / Thùa Thiên 177
Beer Barrel
Black Horse
Hattiesburg
Cocoa Beach
Red Ball VI
Utah / Lien Ket 26 [Link 26]
Waikiki

Boston
Jim Bowie
Silver City
Los Angeles
Fast Buck
Lien Ket 66 [Link 66]
Salem
Tampa (1966)
Buchanan / Wyatt Earp / Kam IV
Honolulu
Wyatt Earp
Wheaton
Palestine
Kings
Oregon
Texas / Lien Ket 28 [Link 28]
Benning
Le Loi 15
Brownsville
Mang Ho V
Brunswick
Olympic
Waycross
Fillmore
Lincoln
Monroe
Jackstay
Su Bok
Buchanan I

Hamilton II / Buchanan II
Red Ball VII
Circle Pines
Indiana / Lien Ket 30 [Link 30]
Alabama
Abilene
Orange
York
Kahuku
Iowa
Toan Thang I
Denver
Austin II
Lam Son 255
Makaha [Ferocious]
Mosby I
Austin
Nevada / Lien Ket 34 [Link 34]
Hot Springs / Lien Ket 36 [Link 36]
Kaena [The Heat]
Kalamazoo
Longfellow
Bolivar
Miami
Kahala
Lexington
Lexington III
Virginia
Yell

Otsego [Clear Water]

Bristol

Omaha

Georgia

Bowie

Chattanooga

Birmingham

Bee Bee

Wyoming

Maili

Miami

Osage

Austin IV

Lihue

Lewis and Clark

Marigold

Cherokee

Davy Crockett

Dexter

Hollingsworth

Montgomery / Lien Ket 40 [Link 40]

Paul Revere / Than Phong 14

Paul Revere III

Warfare

Wayne

Asheville

Limpieza [Cleanup]

Yuma

Crazy Horse / Bun Kae 66-7

Hardihood

Khung Long

Wahiawa

Providence

Carolina Moon

Morgan

Push Ahead

Athens

CHASE (Cut Holes and Sink 'Em) 5

Cheyenne

Mobile

Chicago / Buffalo

Adelaide I

Reno

Adelaide II

Hawthorne / Dan Tang 61

Muskegon

El Paso II

Lam Son 11

Fort Smith

Makiki

Apache

Benning II

Joliet

Adelaide III

Hollandia

Perth

Florida

Hooker I

Mexicali
Santa Fe (1966)
Longstreet
Helemano
Deckhouse I
Nathan Hale
Ehu
Enoggera
Lam Son 283
Yorktown
Beauregard
Coco Palms
Jay / Lam Son 284
Oakland / Lien Ket 46 [Link 46]
Benning III
Holt / Lam Son 286
Henry Clay
Kahana [Turning Point]
James Bond
Macon
Sydney I
Springfield
Washington
Hastings / Deckhouse I
Ewa
Aurora I
Poamoho
El Paso III
Fresno / Quảng Ngãi

Kansas

Kokuliea

Sidney I

Sydney II

Brisbane

Deckhouse II

Aurora II

Cedar Rapids

Dodge

Hayes

Lam Son 290

Tally Ho

John Paul Jones

Cedar Rapids II

Koko Head

Hobart I

Watch Logs

Steel Horse VII

Franklin / Lien Ket 50 [Link 50]

Springfield II

CHASE (Cut Holes and Sink 'Em) 6

Hobart II

Latchkey

Benning IV

Oahu

Paul Revere II

Bucks

Prairie

Seamont

Colorado / Lien Ket 52 [Link 52]

Holsworthy

Lahaina

Aiea

Toledo

Stable

Wilcox

Manitowoc

Pink Rose

El Dorado

Suwannee

Mokuliea

Belfast

Gallup

Deckhouse III

Broome

Smithfield

Allegheny

Castine

Huntsville

Ottawa

Amarillo

Pole Star

Darlinghurst

Byrd

Pawnee

Jackson / Lien Ket 54 [Link 54]

Blue Jay

Kipapa

Alice

Cast Iron

Sunset Beach

Troy

Benning v

Decatur

Baton Rouge

Cranston

El Paso

Napa / Lien Ket 65 [Link 65]

Seward

Meadowlark

Bangor

Athol

Cannon

Pawnee II

Seaside

Vaucluse

Wilton

Thayer I

Atlantic City

Oliver Wendell Holmes

Attleboro

Lanikai [Heavenly Sea]

Danbury

Deckhouse IV

Kalihi

Wren

Kamuela

Batten Down

Casula

Haeng Ho 6

Longview

SLAM (Seeking, Locating, Annihilating and
Monitoring)

Coffee

Boyd

Sioux City

Kathy

Monterey

Benning VI

Crowsnest

Monterey II

Irving / Dai Bang 800 / Operation Mang Ho 6 [72]

Kern

Little Rock

Ostrich

Bathurst

Lam Son 318

Lee / Lien Ket 64 [Link 64]

Canberra

Traffic Cop

Kent

Tulsa

Winchester

Tertib [Order]

Robin

Kailua

Teton

Uniontown (1966–1967)

Craddock

Leeds

Queanbeyan

Shenandoah I

Dover

Duck

Paul Revere IV

Atlanta

Bethlehem

Allentown / Lam Son II South

Madison

Thayer II

Bremerton

Sea Dragon

Adams

Pawnee III

Bundaberg

Geronimo

Travis

Lien Ket 68 [Link 68]

Lanikai II [Heavenly Sea II]

Shasta

Hayman

Yass

Arcadia

Shredder

Dan Tam 81

Canary

Ingham
Rio Blanco / Lien Ket 70 [Link 70]
Waco
Bismark
Charleston
Fort Nisqually
Healdsburg
Mississippi
Fairfax / Rang Dong
Sutter
Ala Moana
Danglesniff
Alexandria
Trinidad
Cortez
Dawn
Trinidad II
Blackjack 22
Lanikai III [Heavenly Sea III]
Sterling
Sierra
Initiator
Glenn
Lanikai IV [Heavenly Sea IV]
Santa Cruz
Shasta II
Chinook I
Wiggins
Nashville

1967

Bratayudha [Bird's Head]

Constitution

Cosh

Garden Plot / The Department of Defense

Civil Disturbance Plan

Handle

Jason

Likewise

Ben Luc

Rustle

Slam

Vanguard

Livid

Sam Houston

Bolo

Glenn Burnie

Kelley Hill

Mang Ho VIII

Niagara Falls

Country Fair 1-25

County Fair

Fitchburg

Niagara (Cedar Falls)

Sunflower

Deckhouse v / Song Than

Garden City

Palm Beach

County Fair 1-28
Silver Lake
Cedar Falls
Caloundra
County Fair 1-29
Dignity
Wollongong
Camden
Lam Son 45
Colby
Pickett
Country Fair 14
County Fair 1-32
Igloo White
Ma Doo I
Stark
Tuscaloosa
Cleveland
Lafayette
Maryland
Farragut
Muncie
Bullseye v
DeSoto
Iola
Seymour
Baek Ma / Whitehorse
Big Spring
Country Fair 1-30

Trinity

Clay

Prairie II

Searcy

Bulkhead

Gadsen

Gatling

Independence

Williston

Tamborine

Muerto Dos [Two Dead]

Green Leaf

Lam Son 67

Beechmont

Dump Truck

Lam Son 46

Stone

Beaumaris

Pershing

Enterprise

Tucson

Dalby

Bunker Hill

Chapman

Deckhouse VI

River Raider I

Bribie

Rio Grande / Lien Ket 81 [Link 81]

Renmark

Chinook II
Suitland
Brandywine
Junction City
Pulaski
Kirribilli
Lanoke
Pittsburg
Sarie Marais
Blackjack 23
Dawes
Knox
Hancock Queen
Oh Jac Kyo I
Waialua
Sapu Bersih [Clean Sweep]
Yuba
Tippecanoe
Blackjack 24
Makalapa
Mop-Up
Prairie III
Beacon Hill
Popeye
Portsea
New Castle
Early
Perry
Hattiesburg (1967)

Summerall

Daniel Boone

Spearhead

Harvest Moon (1967)

Big Horn II

Liberty Blackjack

Canyon

Francis Marion

Dixie

Lejeune

Hop Tac VII

Makalapa II

Oregon (1967)

Dazzlem

Pirous

Humboldt

Blackjack

Blackjack 25

Buckner

Lawrence

Newark

Country Fair 1-34

Prairie V

Golden Fleece 196-1

Kittyhawk

Union I / Lien Ket 102 [Link 102]

Grand

Shawnee

Beau Diddly

Manhattan

Beacon Star

Hancock I

Puckapunyal

Blackjack 33

Beaver Cage

CHASE (Cut Holes and Sink 'Em) 7

Blackjack 41

Fort Wayne

Lismore

Palm Beach II

Hop Tac XVI

Gulf

Leeton

Dayton

Lam Son 48

Bowen

Commando Lava

Malheur I [Misfortune I]

Ahina

Crockett

Kole Kole

Armidale

Webster

Bullard

Hickory / Lam Son 54

Beau Charger

Dallas

Diamond Head

Thunder Dragon

Ashland

Cincinnati

Barking Sands

Duval

Kunia

Waimea

Belt Tight

CHASE (Cut Holes and Sink 'Em) 8

Choctaw

Muitnamah

Union II

Khaled

Cimarron

Hop Tac

Lam Son 63

Cumberland

Bluefield

מוקד [Focus]

Rocket

Tornado

Broken Hill

Colgate

Darwin

Coronado

x-Sundarbans-1

Malheur II [Misfortune II]

Akron

Butler

Kawela

Arizona

Great Bend

Adair

CHASE (Cut Holes and Sink 'Em) 9

Geraldton

Greeley

Brown

Concordia

Cook

Rhino

Billings

Cooparoo

Calhoun

Laggard

Buffalo / Bear Claw

Bear Bite

Riley

Beaver Track

Lion

Lake

March

Paddington

Coronado II / Song Thang 3

Akumu Xay Duong

Fremont

Gem

Crosstie

Hickory II

Goethals

Kingfisher

Ardmore

Beacon Torch

Tiger Concordia VI

Paul Bunyan

Bear Chain / Fremont

Commando Lava II

Pecos

Beacon Guide

Emporia I

Tiger Concordia VIII

Stockton

Tiger Coronado V

Winfield Scott

Pike

Kangaroo Kick

Hood River

Emporia II

Ballarat

Rush

Beacon Gate

Cochise

Родопы [Rhodope]

Benton

Tiger Coronado III

Atherton

Mosman

Emporia III

Beautiful Plum
Coronado IV
Akron II
Tiger Coronado
Burnside
Ulmarra
Belt Drive
Riley II
Yazoo
Tiger Coronado IV
Ainslie
Beacon Point
Valdosta I
Voter
Emporia IV
Swift
Dragon Fire
Muscle Shoals / Dump Truck
Corral
Wheeler / Wallowa
Coronado V
Neutralize
Ballistic Charge
Emporia VI
Fortress Sentry
Arkansas City I
Bolling
Richmond
Shelbyville

Bluefield II

Arkansas City II

Akron III

Shenandoah II

Kenmore

Dazzlem (1967–1968)

Blue Max

Banish Beach

Night Bolt

Beautiful Plum II

Bastion Hill

Coronado VI

Lam Son 138

MacArthur

Medina

Lard Yar

Boudinot

Onslow

Don Ched I

Formation Leader

Tiger Claw

Naresuan

Osceola

Valdosta II

Coronado VII

Voter II

Knox (United States Marine Corps)

Granite

Santa Fe (1967)

Coronado IX
Kentucky
Lancaster I
Neosho
Scotland
Santa Fe (1967–1968)
Napoleon
Essex
Eagle Thrust
Rose
Badger Hunt
Foster
Plaquemines
Kien Giang 9-1
Cove
Strike
Forrest
Ballistic Arch
Sun Devil
Buena Vista
Klamath Falls
Sultan (1967)
Binh Son Support
Canungra
Quicksilver
Tiger Coronado IX
Pitt
Saratoga
Yellowstone

Shepparton
Song Be Contingency
Brush
Citrus
Manchester
Mang Ho IX
Uniontown
Hall
Muscatine
Warm Springs
Piburn
Sylvester
Fortress Ridge
Bold Carousel
Lawley
Badger Tooth
Fargo
Lam Son 166
Auburn

1968

Bannon
Bascote
Clearwater
Eclipse
Embryo
Hecuba
Key Plain

Priam

School Calder

Scoop

Web

Ambush Ally

Niagara

Sultan (1968)

Charcoal

Duntroon

Plumbat

Akron v

Haverford

Altoona

Gator

Uniontown i

San Angelo

Walker

Coronado x

Atalla / Casey

Commando Bolt

Keepout

Lancaster ii

McLain

Neosho ii

Pershing ii

Casey

Jeb Stuart

Niagara ii

Osceola ii

Badger Catch

Red Fox

Coburg

Saline

Adairsville

Lam Son 68

Tran Hung Dao I

Hop Tac I

Uniontown III – Box Springs

Coronado XI

Oakleigh

Mang Ho X

Tran Hung Dao II

Prairie Fire

Houston

Tampa (1968)

Napoleon Saline

Reaction

Patrick

Truong Cong Dinh

Mingo

Coronado XII

Pinnaroo

Show Low

Rock

Harrisburg

Valley Forge

Carentan I

Wilderness

Bolero

Ford

Leap Frog

Quyet Thang / Resolve to Win

Worth

Lam Son 194

Box Springs

San Francisco

Duong Cua Dan

People's Road

Merdeka [Independence]

אסותא [Asuta]

תופת [Inferno]

Los Banos [The Bathroom]

Ashgrove Tram

Woolgoolga

Cochise Green / Dan Sinh

Carentan II

Cooktown Orchid

Pegasus / Lam Son 207

Carlisle

Cranmer

Waterford I

Toan Thang [Complete Victory]

Burlington Trail

Norfolk Victory

Jasper Square

Inferno

Scrotum II

Velvet Hammer

Clifton Corral

Duck Blind

Rice

Delaware / Lam Son 216

Baxter Garden / Lam Son 214

Allons

Houston II

Kudzu

Allen Brook

Concordia Square / Lam Son 224

Golden Valley

Jeb Stuart III

Nevada Eagle

Mameluke Thrust

Truong Cong Dinh [People's Road]

Mathews

Houston III

Toan Thang II [Complete Victory II]

Androcles / Bootstrap

Swift Saber

Banjo Royce / Quang Trung 23/4

CHASE (Cut Holes and Sink 'Em) 11

Kosciusko

Duel Blade

Harmon Green

Norfolk Victory II

Chattahoochee Swamp / Lien Ket 45 [Link 45]

Vance Canyon

Charger / Lam Son 235

Houston IV

Thor

Pocahontas Forest

Hayride

Bowline

Quyet Chien [Fought]

Merino

Oceanside

Swift Play

Platypus

Lyre Bird

Lam Son 245

CHASE (Cut Holes and Sink 'Em) 12

Somerset Plain / Lam Son 246

Nowra

Dodge Valley

Telemachus

Danube

Dan Sinh 22-6 / Population 22-6

Diamantina

Sussex Bay

OAU

Champaign Grove

Innamincka

Commanche Falls I

Vĩnh Lộc [Good Fortune]

Eagle II / Toan Thang 9/68 [Victorious 9/68]

Lam Son 261

Hawkesbury

Sullivan

Golden Sword

Crown

Owen Mesa

Golden Fleece / Lien Ket 60 [Link 60]

Pioneer

Phu Vang I

Sceptre

Windsor

Talladega Canyon

Dukes Glade

Jason

Commanche Falls II

Norwalk

Maui Peak

Logan Field

Sealords

Capital

Lam Son 271

Dale Common

Henderson Hill

Rich

Dawson River Afton

Garrad Bay

Harvest

Phu Vang III

Vernon Lake I

Liberty Canyon
Sabine Draw
הלם [Shock]
Napoleon Saline II
Wintney
Search Turn
Commanche Falls III
Vernon Lake II
Nicollet Bay
Commando Hunt
Sheridan Sabre
Kudzu II
Meade River / Hung Quang 1/81
Piedmont Swift
Aureole
Hardin Falls
Speedy Express
Goodwood
Giant Slingshot
Taylor Common
Le Loi I
Marshall Mountain
King Hit
Phu Vang IV
Fayette Canyon
Navaho Warhorse I
Valiant Hunt
Rawlings Valley
Boundary Rider

תשורה [Gift]
Todd Forest

1969

Knuckle

Loxwood

Madrigal

Prologue

Sheepskin

Wig

Quyet Thang II [Resolve to Win II]

Rice Farmer

Skysweep

Barrier Reef

Tiger Balm

Water Trap

Big Muddy

Caloundra

Treasure Island

Russell Beach

Bold Mariner

Chaos

Toan Thang 1/69 [Complete Victory 1/69]

Dewey Canyon

Wheeler Place

Ohio Rapids

Sherman Peak

Arlington

Linn River
Darby Crest
Greene Blue
Greene Thunder
Hancock Knight
Putnam Panther
Wayne Arrow
Hines
Greene Queen
Wayne Dart
Darby Trail II
Hancock Eagle
Cheyenne Sabre
Strangler I
Greene Cyclone
Wayne Green
Strangler II
Navaho Warhorse II
Sea Tiger
Toan Thang III [Complete Victory III]
Spokane Rapids
Greene Tornado
Purple Martin / Massachusetts Bay
Quảng Nam
Greene Thunder II
Iron Mountain
Kentucky Jumper
Massachusetts Striker
Oklahoma Hills

Quintus Thrust

Wayne Grey

Darby Crest II

Stingray I

Federal / Overlander

Maine Crag

Stingray II

Lulu

Commando Vault

Darby Crest III

Darby March

Remagen

Rain Dance

Atlas Wedge

Frederick Hill

Geneva Park

Menu

Anguilla / Sheepskin

Greene Hurricane

Montana Mauler

Clarksville

Hancock Eagle III

Hancock Knight II

Cane Field

Montana Scout

Overland

Hancock Knight III

Ellis Ravine

Muskogee Meadow

Overlander
Atlas Power
Beaver Dam
Deerstalk
Montana Raider
Wayne Javelin
Bison
Greene Orange
Washington Green
Putnam Tiger
Greene Typhoon
Stafford
Dan Thang 69
Dan Tien 33D
Greene Lion
Lam Son 277
Surfside
Massachusetts Bay
Bristol Boots
Greene Queen II
Virginia Ridge
Hybrid
Mailed Fist
Greene Orange II
Twickenham
Greene Orange III
Greene Typhoon II
Herkimer Mountain
Reynella

Apache Snow

Roadside

Dan Quyen 38-A [People's Right 38-A]

Green Basket

Lamar Plain

Greene Gallop

Twickenham II

Pipestone Canyon

Cameron Falls

Lavarack

Montgomery Rendezvous

Tong

Utah Mesa

Esso

Iroquois Grove

Green Ax

Kentucky Cougar

Tennessee Pride

Sea Float / Solid Anchor/ Tran Hung Dao III

Matthew

Forsythe Grove

Arlington Canyon

Campbell Steamer

Williams Glade

Mundingburra

Gaffey Base

Greene Jack

Georgia Tar

Mandrel

Ginger

Hat Dich

Bulmus 6 / Green Island Raid

Boxer 1

Durham Peak

Nantucket Beach

Boxer 2

Strangle 1

Idaho Canyon

Boxer 3

Boxer 4

Boxer 5

Boxer 6

Nutcracker

Platypus (1969)

Red Hat

Green Ace

Cumberland Thunder

Banner

Carolina Blaster

Grenada

Richland Square

Claiborne Chute

Louisiana Lee

Nepabunna

Bull Run 1

Lien Ket 414 [Link 414]

Lien Ket 531 [Link 531]

Burnham

Chieftain

Defiant Stand

Escort

רביב [Drizzle]

Wayne Boulder

Kingston

Keystone Cardinal

Putnam Cougar

Hancock Flame

Republic Square

Norton Falls

Darby Trail III

Saturate

Hartle Green

Ross

Cramer White

Greene Bear

Wayne Breaker

Greene Bullet

Hodges Black

Cliff Dweller

Fulton Square

Union Square

Kings Cross

Monopoly

Putnam Wildcat

Toan Thang IV [Complete Victory IV]

Spragins White

Wayne Rock

Dan Tien 40
Bertrand
While Away
Ransom Raider
Texas Traveller
Waldron Blue
Marsden
Hughes Black
Long Reach II
Randolph Glen
Vintage Rally
Tangle
Noa
Rooster 53
Bondi I
Bondi II

1970

Baytown
Jersey Bombs
Leopard
Median
Pisces
Yukon
Cliff Dweller IV
Lunch
Wayne Thrust
Flying Finn

Snack

Priha 1 [Blossom 1]

Dinner

Dessert

Napier

Supper

Priha 2 [Blossom 2]

Matilda

Priha 3 [Blossom 3]

Putnam Power

Bull Run II

Green River

רודוס [Rhodes]

Keperra

Priha 4 [Blossom 4]

Priha 5 [Blossom 5]

Fresh Start

Greene Deuce

Putnam Shark

Wayne Stab

York Market

Keystone Blue Jay

Hammersley

Priha 6 [Blossom 6]

Priha 7 [Blossom 7]

Priha 8 [Blossom 8]

Dakota Clint

Priha 9 [Blossom 9]

Priha 10 [Blossom 10]

Goodlook

Priha 11 [Blossom 11]

Gisborne

Park Silver / Hancock Dragon

Hamilton

Priha 12 [Blossom 12]

Finschhafen

Earhart White

Darby Talon

Priha 14 [Blossom 14]

Eichelberger Black

Good Luck

Priha 15 [Blossom 15]

Townsville

Graphic Hand

Priha 16 [Blossom 16]

Priha 17 [Blossom 17]

Patio

Texas Star

Priha 18 [Blossom 18]

Tat Thang 18

Phoi Hop [Combination]

Priha 19 [Blossom 19]

Priha 20 [Blossom 20]

Priha 21 [Blossom 21]

Toan Thang 41 [Complete Victory 41]

Concrete 1

Nudgee

Baird Silver

Cambodian Incursion

Toan Thang 42 [Complete Victory 42]

Plateau

Platte Canyon

Dong Tien II [Coin II] / Toan Thang 43
  [Complete Victory 43]

Rockcrusher

Upshot

Fishhook

Binh Tay I [Infantry Arms I]

Bold Lancer I

Cavalier Beach

Toan Thang 44 [Complete Victory 44]

Toan Thang 45 [Complete Victory 45]

Toan Thang 46 [Complete Victory 46]

Toan Thang 500 [Complete Victory 500]

Concrete II

Cuu Long [Mekong]

Binh Tay II [Infantry Arms II]

Cheadle Blue

Padlock

Ashfield

Barbara Glade I

Bold Lancer II

Wayne Jump

Cuu Long II [Mekong II]

Fredenhall Gold

Putnam Paragon

Freedom Deal

Binh Tay III [Infantry Arms III] / Tame The West
Bryan White
Cuu Long III [Mekong III]
Capricorn
Robertson White
Wayne Hurdle
Cung Chung 1 [We Together 1]
Hancock Hawk
Elanora
Barbara Glade II
Binh Tay IV [Infantry Arms IV]
Wayne Fast
Wright Blue
Clemens Green
Birdwood
Pennsylvania Square
Petrie
Character
Keystone Robin (Alpha)
Brandeis Blue
Hancock Gold
Nó Górdio [Gordion Knot]
Clinch Valley
Elk Canyon
Nathan
Pickens Forest
Wayne Span I
Wolfe Mountain
Decade

Barren Green

Chicago Peak

Brandeis Blue II

Lyon Valley

Greene Jack (1970)

Wayne Span II

רימון 20 [Pomegranate 20]

Kavkaz

CHASE (Cut Holes and Sink 'Em) 10

Cung Chung 2 [We Together 2]

Wayne Pierce

Comeback Ridge

Ripley Center

Chenla 1

Wayne Forge

Massey-Harris

Imperial Lake

Jefferson Glenn / Texas Star

Nebraska Rapids

Ballard Valley

Cung Chung 3 [We Together 3]

Tailwind

Catawba Falls

Dubois Square

Murray Blue

Tiger Mountain

Pimlico

Project Delta

Tolare Falls 1

Wayne Sabre
Putnam Valley
Emery
Keystone Robin (Bravo)
Noble Canyon
Tolare Falls II
Burlap
Hickman
Zebra 3
Hancock Dragon
Ivory Coast
Kingpin
Mar Verde [Green Sea]
Darby Swing
Hoang Dieu 101

1971

Backscratch
Greene Lightning
Greene Storm
Keystone Robin (Charlie)
Omega
Performance
Upshur Stream
Lam Son 719
Dewey Canyon II
Hoang Dieu 103
Attune

Finney Hill

Middlesex Peak

Bright Light

Wasco Rapids

Greene Sure

Searchlight

Great Fly-In

Montana Mustang

Lam Son 720

Barisal

Caroline Hill

200

Keystone Oriole (Alpha)

Jackpot

Granite

सफेद सागर / White Sea

Blue Bottle

Overlord

Grommet

Keystone Oriole (Bravo)

Demetrius

Chenla II

Keystone Oriole (Charlie)

41 / Granite Two

Lam Son 810

Katum

Jaguar

Mantling

Galaxy

Hotpants
Halibut
Hamish
Danger
Keystone Mallard
Cactus Lilly
Chengiz Khan
Trident
Python
Ectoblast
Faldage
Galantine

1972

Dhib
Marble
Keystone Owl
Putney
Prek Ta
Seahawk
Eastertide: Quang Tri
Freedom Train
Eastertide: An Loc
Bullet Shot
Constant Guard I
Constant Guard II
Eastertide: Kon Tum
Keystone Pheasant

Plathond
Pocket Money
Isotope
Linebacker I
Constant Guard III
Koteka
Thunderhead
Keystone Wren
Folklore
Pacer IVY / Pacer Inventory
Toggle
Ticky
Motorman
Keystone Pelican
Boulder
Constant Guard IV
זעם האל [Wrath of God] / Bayonet
Waverider
Zealous
Marosca
Linebacker II

1973

End Sweep
Homecoming
Bloodstone
Khana Cascade
Yarrow

Spring of Youth

Claymore

Arbor

بدر [Badr]

דוגמן 5 [Model 5]

כתונת [Shift]

Nickel Grass

א בירי לב [Knights Heart] / Gazelle

קינוח [Dessert]

Interknit

1974

Aroma III

Audacity

Colombo

Gulf

Intrench

Jamb / Jeroboam

Sea Lion

Storm

Nimbus Star

Nimbus Moon

Derringer

Dylan

Infringe

Nimrod Spar

Danaca

Bedrock

Atilla / Cyprus Peace / 1974 Peace
Niki
Jackson
Rheostat
Dirk
Grenada
Navy Help Darwin

1975

Da Yu
Rampart
Slant
Pagoda
Satrap
New Life
Eagle Pull
Frequent Wind
Gading
Mila
Nimbus Stream
Feature
Poplar
Sausage II
Heliotrope
Flamboyan [Flamboyant]
Anvil
Primicia [Scoop]
Morgan

Savannah
Carlota
Cóndor [Condor]
Independencia [Independence]
Komodo
Poinciana
Seroja / Lotus

1976

Agila
Fluid Drive
Entebbe / Thunderbolt
Enshroud
Eland
Tenable
Fulcrum
Pacer HO (Pacer Herbicide Orange)
Seiljag / Yacht
Cenderawasih

1977

Kikis [Rub Out]
Quadrant
Tybalt
Verveine [Verbena]
Fair Play
Strenuous

Rising Sun

Pico [Peak]

Kropduif [Cropper]

Feuerzauber [Magic Fire]

Cresset

Bravado

Charly

Dingo

Prato [Plate]

Lamantin [Manatee]

1978

Eyesore

Oilsafe

Via Satcom

SETCON I (Set Consolidation I)

Morning Light

Athene

Naga Min Sitsin Yae [King Dragon]

Tacaud [Pout]

Midlink

Sphinx

Litani

Angora

Reindeer

Léopard / Bonite [Bonito]

Red Bean

Campus

Rextill
Gatling
Quicksilver
Soberanía / Sovereignty

1979

Vanity
Elf One (European Liaison Force One)
Rekstok
Safraan [Saffron]
Priha 13 [Blossom 13]
Abalone
Houari Boumedienne
Cyclone
Culex
Barracuda
Dice
Tinderbox
Agila
Midford
Agat
Шторм-333 [Storm-333]

1980

Balloon
Commonsense
Gateway

Shiraro

Merger

Quartz

Hectic

Panjshir I

Eagle Claw / Evening Light / Rice Bowl

بیتالمقدس [Jerusalem]

Nimrod

SETCON II (Set Consolidation II)

Ranger

Tiro a Tiro [Shot Shot]

Thrasher

Hurricane

Sceptic

Titan

Lash

Vastrap [Traction]

Repulse

Grapple

Klipklop

Splinter

Tangent

Bright Star

Kaman 99 [Bow 99]

شمشیر سوزان [Scorch Sword]

Aroma 11

Panjshir II

Guardian

سلطان ۰۱ [Sultan 10]

Scarab

Scarab Minor

عملیات مروارید [Morvarid / Pearl]

Exercise Creek Sentry

1981

Vasbyt [Hang in There]

Nasr [Victory]

Beanbag

Carnation

Panjshir III

Galang Support

Attack on H3

Pagar Betis [Fence of Legs]

РЯН [Raketno-Yadernoe Napadenie] / RYaN
    [Nuclear Missile Attack]

Contraguerrilla Machete / Counterinsurgency
    Machete

אופרה [Opera] / Babylon

Rocky Mountain Transfer

Ceniza [Ashes]

Konyn [Rabbit]

Protea

Panjshir IV

Keamanan [Security]

Ash 81

عملیات ثامن‌الائمه [Eighth Imam]

Praetorian

Daisy

طريق القدس [Jerusalem Way]

Kerslig [Candle Light]

1982

Retorno

Bonanza

Red Star

Super

al-Fawz al-'Azim [Supreme Success]

فتحالمبين [Undeniable Victory]

Corporate

Rosario

Yahoo

Paraquet

Black Buck One

Black Buck Two

Panjshir V

Plum Duff

Mikado

Sutton

Autoimpuesta [Self-Imposed]

Black Buck Five

Black Buck Six

Victoria 82

של"ג [Peace for Galilee]

ערצב 19 [Mole Cricket 19]

Black Buck Seven

Keyhole

Hurricane

Ramadan

Sofia

Mebos

Panjshir VI

Épaulard I [Orca I]

Mazurka

Muslim ibn Aqil

Muharram

Ixil

Phalanx

1983

Drama

Fajr al-Nasr [Before the Dawn] / Dawn of
    Victory

Firmeza 83 [Firmness 83]

Phoenix

Early Call

Valfajr 1 [Dawn 1]

Dolfyn [Dolphin]

Skerwe [Scissors]

Infektion [Infection]

Valfajr 2 [Dawn 2]

Patuca

Valfajr 3 [Dawn 3]

Manta

Arid Farmer
Millstone
Valfajr 4 [Dawn 4]
Urgent Fury
Askari
Fusileer
Island Breeze

1984

Candrasa
Valfajr 5 [Dawn 5]
Kheibar
Valfajr 6 [Dawn 6]
मेघदूत [Cloud Messenger]
Panjshir VII
Metal
Blue Star
Shop
Tupac
Woodrose
عملیات بیت‌المقدس [Jerusalem 2]
Hsing Kuang [Starlight]
Intense Look
Panjshir VIII
Grenadier
משה [Moses]
Joshua / Sheba
Lemon

1985

Lifeline-Tete Corridor
Congresso II
Badr [Full Moon]
Magneto
Argon / Cabinda
Plecksy
Plexi
Panjshir IX
Boswilger
Grape Fruit
Calumet
Weldmesh [Wallpaper]
Bordkante [The Border's Edge]
Egret
רגל עץ [Wooden Leg]
Charioteer
Ghost Rider

1986

Octopus
Attain Document
Valfajr 8 [Dawn 8]
Attain Document II
Épervier [Sparrowhawk]
الأنفال [Spoils of War]
Attain Document III

El Dorado Canyon
Black Thunder
Kodak
Blast Furnace
Southern Cross
Alpha Centauri
Западня [Trap]
Гератских [Herati]
Karbala-3
Musketeer
Colosseum
Brasstacks
Karbala-4

1987

Karbala-5
Karbala-6
Karbala-7
Karbala-9
Rolio
Karbala-10
Nasr-4
Falcon
Morris Dance
光谱 [Spectrum]
Vadamarachchi [Liberation]
பூமாலை [Garland of Flowers]
Rajiv [Wind]

Earnest Will
Eager Glacier
Prime Chance
Moduler
Coolidge
Pawan [Wind]
Nimble Archer
Touchstone
Firewood
Magistral
Saludando Octubre [Saluting October]
Bushmaster

1988

Bandit
Hooper
Catch and Kill / Sadhbhavna [Goodwill]
Danto
Flavius
Golden Pheasant
Packer
Zafar 7 [Victory 7]
Trishul [Trident]
वराट [Giant]
Ramadan Mubarak [Blessed Ramadan]
توكلنا على الله [In God we Trust]
Praying Mantis
Displace

Prone

Black Thunder II

Red Bean

Linger

Agree

Checkmate

Mount Hope III

چهل چراغ [Forty Stars]

Katzen

Forough Javidan [Eternal Light]

Mersad [Ambush]

Vuiswys

Cornerstone

Cactus

Marion

1989

Prayer Book / Elaborate Maze

Тайфу́н [Typhoon]

Adwa

Midnight Jackal

Unique

Matador

Amazing

Merlyn

Lifeline Sudan

Jaring Merah [Red Net]

Nimrod Dancer / Nimrod Sustain

Blade Jewel
Purple Storm
Sand Flea
Aksum
Keystone Eagle
Uhai [Life]
Беремот [Behemoth]
Hawkeye
Hugo
Aqueduct
Classic Resolve
Sultan
Acid Gambit
Blue Spoon / La Invasión / Just Cause
Nifty Package

1990

Missing in Action Stingers
Samum / Simoom
Corymbe / Highbush
Blind Logic / Promote Liberty
Fenkil
Ashaka Sena [Ashka Army]
Conservation
Gajasinghe
Steel Box / Golden Python
Desert Shield
Friction

Granby
Locusta [Locust]
Sharp Edge
Artimon [Mizzen]
Anchor Guard
Salon
Salamandre [Salamander]
Sea Breeze
Damask I
Thrividha Balaya
Green Beam
Noroît [Northwest Wind]
Scimitar
Heritage
Jayasakthi
Sculpin
Imminent Thunder
Damask II

1991

Eastern Exit
Ace Guard
Alfil [Bishop]
Scalpel
Daguet [Brocket Deer]
Desert Storm / Instant Thunder
Desert Sting
Vengeful

Bedem [Ditch]

Proven Force

Desert Sword / Desert Sabre

Trebor

Desert Farewell / Desert Calm/ Peace Walker

Raskelja

Bronze

Genesis

North

Haven

Provide Comfort

Silencio [Silence]

Libage [Quarry Stone]

Airone [Heron]

Forum

Assist

Python

Кольцо I [Ring I]

Rockingham

Blue Lodge

Record

Кольцо II [Ring II]

Positive Force

Pyi Thaya [Clean and Beautiful Nation]

Sea Angel [Productive Effort]

Habitat

Jaring Merah II [Red Nets 2]

שלמה [Solomon]

Pastel

Fiery Vigil

Damask III

Jural

Match

Provide Promise

Balavegaya [Power Force]

Provide Comfort II

Žalac/ Žaoka [Stinger]

Беремот-2 [Behemoth 2]

Labrador

Opera Orientalis / Opera

Vukovar [Thunder]

Lightning

Baumier [Balsam]

Blue Beam

Bolster

Obala-91 [Coast-91]

Balavegaya II [Power Force II]

Victor Squared

Quick Lift

Bilogora

Julin

Boxtop

Otkos 10 [Swath 10]

Marquis

Safe Harbour

Papuk-91

Strela [Arrow]

Orkan 91 [Hurricane 91]

Vihor [Whirlwind]

1992

Cleansing

Loren

Provide Hope I

Allied Goodwill I

Allied Goodwill II

Harmony

Baranja [Requests]

Provide Hope II

Somalia I

Silver Anvil

Agile Genie

Wedding in the Mountains

Gypsy

Cavtat [Scorched Earth]

Jaguar

Čagalj [Jackal] / Lipanjske Zore [June Dawns]

Врбас 92 [Vrbas 92]

Goranboy

Коридор 92 [Corridor 92]

Clean-up / Blue Fox

Miljevci

Solania

Tigar / Tiger

Cavalier

Maritime Monitor

Oslobođena zemlja / Liberated Land

Eager Mace

Provide Relief

Provide Transition

Relief

Southern Watch

Bolton

Kuzey Irak / Northern Iraq

Grapple

Sky Monitor

Vlaštica / Privileges

Maritime Guard

Deliverance

Restore Hope

Consonance

Oryx

1993

Sunny Winter

Driftnet

Able Manner

Maslenica

Peruča

Afshar

Chimère et Volcan [Chimera and Volcano]

Provide Refuge

Provide Hope III

Albatross

Somalia II

Deny Flight

Continue Hope

Tosca
Bajoyer [Lock Wall]
Sharp Guard
Sharp Vigilance
Lance
Able Sentry
Accountability
Golden Fleece
Neretva 93
Gothic Serpent
Medački džep [Medak Pocket]
Cauldron
Forward Action
Chitedze (Velvet Bean)
Bwezani (Give Back)
Solace
Pauk [Spider]
Clean Corridor

1994

Arco Iris [Rainbow]
Provide Hope IV
Ippocampo [Hippocampus]
Distant Runner
Skok 1 [Leap 1]
Amaryllis
Silver Back
Bøllebank [Hooligan Bashing]

Quick Draw

Diapason [Tuning Fork]

Tiger Rescue

Insecticide

Diapason II [Tuning Fork II]

Tigar 94 [Tiger 94]

Skok 2 [Leap 2]

Turquoise

Coracle

Support Hope

Tamar

Sea Signal

Able Vigil

Cadence

Safe Haven

Uphold Democracy / Restore Democracy

Lagoon

Vigilant Warrior

Jesen-94 [Autumn-94]

Amanders

Grmec

Cinciar

Winter 94 [Zima 94]

1995

United Shield

Safe Border

Safe Passage

Çelik [Steel]

New Horizons

Блесак [Flash]

Good Samaritan

Unified Endeavor

Marathon Pacific

Криваја 95 [Krivaja 95]

Quicklift

Leap Forward

Prompt Return 95

Stupčanica 95

Kilpi-95 [Shield-95]

Miekka-95

Ljeto 95 [Summer 95]

Олуја [Storm]

Deadeye

Deliberate Force

Mistral I

Mistral II

Una

Thunder Strike

Burin

Azalée [Azalea]

Južni Potez [Southern Transfer]

Sana

Riviresa [Sunrays]

Vigilant Sentinel

Zorro II

Century

Alliance
Firm Endeavour
Joint Endeavour

1996

Chaperon
Save Sua
Assured Response
ענבי זעם [Grapes of Wrath]
Almandin I [Almandine I]
Mosby II
Mbata [Immigration]
Almandin II [Almandine II]
Quick Response
Standard
Sath Jaya I [Taken Together I]
Sath Jaya II [Taken Together II]
Desert Strike
Sath Jaya III [Taken Together III]
Lodestar
Stable
Joint Falcon
Guardian Assistance / Assurance / Phoenix
Tusk
Decisive Endeavor
Joint Guard
Pyramid

1997

Black Fox
Northern Watch
Vision
Osier
Present Haven
Assured Lift
Silver Wake
Libelle [Dragonfly]
Guardian Retrieval
White Flags
Alba [Sunrise]
Green Stream
Chavín de Huántar
Assistance
Çekiç [Hammer]
Jayasikurui [Certain Victory]
Sure Victory
Noble Obelisk
Firm Response
Bevel Edge
Constable
Cranberry
Şafak [Dawn]
Bel Isi
Mandarin
Compliment / Present Haven

1998

Recuperation
Noble Response
Solar Sunrise
Stanhope
Determination
Pollard
Prudence
Murat
Excite / Hilti / Prone
Bevel Incline
Shakti [Power]
Chagai-ı
Chagai-ıı
Quartz
Safe Departure
Shepherd Venture
Determined Falcon
Joint Forge
Потковица [Horseshoe]
Kitona
Vagabond
Resolute Response
Infinite Reach
Persistence
Boleas
Shadow Express
Eagle Eye

Central

Sovereign Legitimacy

Badr [Full Moon]

Joint Guarantor / Determined Guarantor

Fuerte Apoyo [Strong Support]

Rivibala [Rivi Force]

Desert Fox

Spartic

Climate Change

1999

Satgas Wibawa [Authority]

Preamble

Sadar Rencong [Beware of the Dagger]

Rana Gosa [Battle Cry]

Module

Allied Force / Noble Anvil / Merciful Angel

Echo

Kinetic

Sapu Jagad [Total Cleansing]

वजिय [Victory]

Talwar [Sword]

Augmentation

Joint Guardian

KFOR (Kosovo Force)

Concord

Faber

Sadar Rencong II [Beware of the Dagger II]

Torrent

Avid Response

Spitfire

Toucan

Stabilise

Warden

Crocodile

Desert Spring

Rapid Guardian

Wiradharma / Guntur

Reptile

Fundamental Response

Abacus

2000

Sadar Rencong III [Beware the Dagger III]

Merlin

Lichi

Silent Promise / Atlas Response

Tanager

Palliser

Basilica

Khukri

Megaphone

Artisan

Focus Relief I

Barras

Kinihira I

Kinihira ii
Quadrant
Kinihira iii
Addition
Trek
Sculpture
Kinihira iv
Husky
Espresso
Eclipse
Kinihira v
Kinihira vii
Kinihira viii

2001

New Horizons
Kinihira ix
Pomelo
River City
Sirius
Teebone
Harpoon
Balboa
Santorini
Humble
Agni Kheela [Fireball]
Focus Relief ii
Celesta

Essential Harvest

Forage

Rivikirana

Relentless Strike

Yellow Ribbon

Support

Noble Eagle

Focus Relief III

Infinite Justice / Enduring Freedom

Amber Fox

Relex

Active Endeavour

Crescent Wind

Veritas

Apollo

Enduring Freedom – Afghanistan

Eagle Assist

Rhino

Héraclès

Trent

Slipper

Parakram [Valour]

Enduring Freedom – Kyrgyzstan

2002

Fingal

Liberation

תיבת נוח [Noah's Ark]

Enduring Freedom – Philippines / Freedom Eagle

Sutton

Avid Recovery

Anaconda

Iron Fist

Relex II

Glock

חומת מגן [Defensive Shield]

Jacana

Palladium

Ptarmigan

Snipe

Tanker Two

Citadel

Torii

Enduring Freedom – Pankisi Gorge

Polar Harpoon

Condor

Buzzard

Narwhal

Herrick

Southern Focus

Rencong Terbang [Flying Dagger]

דרך נחושה [Determined Path]

Grizzly

Asperges [Asparagus]

Romeo-Sierra

Mountain Sweep

Oracle

Licorne [Unicorn]

Autumn Return

Enduring Freedom – Horn of Africa

Boali

Shepherd Sentry

Bali Assist

Accius

Allied Harmony

2003

Mistral

Headstrong

Tsunami

Bastille

Eagle Fury

Mountain Viper

Epidote

Display Deterrence

Mass Appeal

Solitude

Iraqi Freedom

Iraqi Liberation

Telic

Falconer

Fusion

Northern Delay

Viking Hammer

Concordia
Airborne Dragon
Option North
Palate
Pebu [Shelter]
Terpadu [Integrated]
Planet x
Libertad Uno [Freedom One]
Caravan
Peninsula Strike
Providence
Shining Express
Artemis
Desert Snowplough
Desert Scorpion
Scorpion Sting
Spartan Scorpion
Sparviero [Sparrowhawk]
Arès [Aries]
Sidewinder
Tyr
Haven Denial
Iron Bullet
Soda Mountain
14 Juillet [14 July]
Antica Babilonia [Ancient Babylon]
Ivy Serpent
White House
Athena

Warrior Sweep

Tapeworm

Anode / Helpem Fren

Peregrine

Ivy Lightning

Silverado

Ivy Needle

Gemsbok

Longstreet

Nibbio [Kite]

Liane

Industrial Sweep

Desert Thrust

Montego

Tiger Clean Sweep

Chamberlain

Sweeny

O.K. Corral

All-American Tiger

Armadillo

Ivy Cyclone

Mountain Resolve

Boothill

Eagle Curtain

Buford

Matraqa Hadidia [Iron Hammer]

Ivy Cyclone II

Rifles Blitz

Rifle Sweep

Bayonet Lightning
Bulldog Mammoth
Clear Area
Abilene
Panther Squeeze
Red Dawn
Panther Backroads
All Clear
Proxima
Arrowhead Blizzard
Ivy Blizzard
Iron Justice
Rifles Fury
Devil Siphon
Overcoat
Salam
Santa Strike
Iron Force
Iron Grip
Benin / Cotonou
Choke Hold

2004

Gimlet Victory
I CAN
Northern Wind
Altair
Mountain Blizzard

Iron Resolve
Clothes for Kids
Market Sweep
Saloon
Warhorse Whirlwind
Centaur Fast Gas
Rock Slide
Wolfhound Trap II
Wolfhound Fury II
Wolverine Feast
Final Cut
Tomahawk
Trailblazer
Topaz
Saber Turner II
Eagle Liberty 3
Devil Clinch
Rocketman
Secure Tomorrow
Warrior
Soccer Ball
Hickory View
Devil Thrust
Aloha
Shillelagh
Suicide Kings
Iron Promise
Centaur Rodeo
Hacurri No. 1

Hacurri No. 2
Iron Saber
Lancer Lightning
Duke Fortitude
Lancer Fury
Vigilant Resolve
Resolute Sword
JM
Danger Fortitude
Ripper Sweep
Yellow Stone
Striker Hurricane
Spring Cleanup
Thunderstruck
Wolfpack Crunch
Arrrowhead Strike 10
Rapier Thrust
Student to Student
קשת בענן [Rainbow]
Disarm
Spire
Diyala Border Police Audit
Celtics
Halo
Asbury Park
Ashbury Park II
Slim Shady
Striker Tornado
Giuliani

Tusker Sand

Carbet

Rocketman III

Asperges 2 [Asparagus 2]

Safari

Distinguished Games

Dragon Victory

Gimlet Crusader

Haifa Street

Lightning Resolve

Mutual Security

Phantom Linebacker

Gimlet Silent Sniper

Cordite

Oasis

Outlaw Destroyer

School House

Tombstone Piledriver

Flashman

Mayfield III

Cobra Sweep

Dorca

Dragon Tree

Quarterhouse Rides

Tiger Care

Warrior Resolve

Cajun Mousetrap II

Cajun Mousetrap III

Iron Fury

Iron Fury II
Showdown
Wolverine
Grizzly Forced Entry
Clean Sweep
True Grit
Hurricane
Black Typhoon
Hurricane II
Iron Fist II
Longhorn
Marne
Predator
ימי תשובה [Days of Penitence]
Backpack
Iolaus
Tangerine Pinch
Mustang Flex
Wolfhound Fury
Bulldog
Ramadan Roundup
Centaur Strike II
Centaur Strike III
Mandarin Squeeze
Mustang Socko
Tiger Club
Tangerine Squeeze
Crayon
Duliyah Sunrise

Dallas
Tiger Fury
Army Santa
Duke Fury
Al Fajr [New Dawn]
Phantom Fury
Windy City
Phillis
Wolfhound Power
Wolfhound Jab
Rock Bottom
Plymouth Rock
Althea
Tobruk
Bima [Get Out]
Baton Rouge
Boreas
Falcon Freedom
Soprano Sunset
Maguta
Iraqi Children
Astrée [Astrea]
Backbreaker
Lion Cub
Wonderland
Unified Assistance
Castor
Madad [Help]
Rainbow

Sea Waves
Sumatra Assist
Powder River
Triple Play

2005

Attleboro
Dunlap
East Lansing
Hudson
Moving Forward
Neighborhood Watch
Spider Web
River Walk
Structure
Moon
Power Geyser
Tsunami Assist
Taguta Sisuthi [Eat Well]
Proteus
Lanthonid
Therapist
Gambhir [Serious]
Hedgehog
Sea Wave
Vacant City
Copperas Cove
Keystone Sweep

Checkmate

Big Dig

Spurs

Catalyst

Centaur Showdown

River Blitz

Al Barkh [Lightning]

River Bridge

Mavericks

Unforgiven

Azure

Swashbuckle

Outer Banks

יד לאחים [Giving Brothers a Hand]

Fontana

Falcon (Federal and Local Cops Organized
    Nationally) I

Block Party

Grey Wolf II

Murambatsvina [Drive Out Rubbish] / Restore
    Order

Badlands

Scrimmage

Vigilance

Clear Decision

Cobweb

Matador

Quicksweep

Block Party II

Mongoose
Dragons Breath
Peninsula
Chiron
Squeeze Play
Chepultepec
Souk Jadeed [New Market]
Moon River Dragon
San Juan
Tarnished Eagle
Uhaser
Woodstock
Pitchfork
Romhe [Spear]
White Shield
Khanjar [Strike of the Sword]
Nilo [Nile]
Red Wings II
al Azil al Sitrateegi [Strategic Separation]
Diablo Reach Back
Palate II
Red Wings
Saif [Sword]
Shadyville
Demon Digger
Seahorse
Thunder
Muthana Strike
Sergeant Thea'a

Bow Country

Hunter / Sayaid

Scimitar

Archer

Augural

Marlborough

Firework Fanfare

Warrior's Rage

Whalers

Quick Strike

Able Warrior

Vanguard Thunder

Hudson Sentinel

Restoring Rights

Pizmah

Gladius

Argus

Zoba's [Cyclone]

Flea Flicker

Unison

National Unity

Rose Bowl

Carentan

Clydesdale

Kabda Bil Hadid [Iron Fist]

Bowie

Saratoga

Hiba [Mountaineers]

River Gate / Bawwabatu Annaher

Pakistan Assist

Winter Race

Fiesta Bowl

Plateau

Pil

Constitution Hammer

Doctor

Canopy

Cornhusker

Harba [Shank]

Teutonic

Great Lakes

Al Hajip Elfulathi [Steel Curtain]

Syrian Round-up

Wolf Stalk II

Slapshot

Open Window

Fiesta Bowl II

Knockout

Paradise City II

Kennesaw Dragon

Home Run

Bruins / Dibbah

Cotton Bowl

Asad [Lions]

Numur [Tigers]

Tyche Round-up

Turkey Bowl

Tallie [Rams]

Stocking Stuffer
Gashshaa [Skinner]
Able Rising Force
Bull Dawg Chariot
Sleigh Ride
Liberty Express
Green Trident

2006

Counterstrike
Post Hawk
Sextant
Red Bull
Unified Fist
Falcon Sweep
Red Bull II
Koa Canyon / Wadi Aljundi
Baghdad is Beautiful
King Tut
Al Dharba Al Nihaa'ya [Final Strike]
Smokewagon
Wide Receiver
Pit Bull
Ala Allah [God Help Us]
Dirty Harry
Minotaur
El Toro Loco
Glory Light

Jaws v

Swamp Fox

Mr. Rogers' Neighborhood

Rampart Lion I

Focus

Scales of Justice

הבאת ביכורים [Bringing Home the Goods]

Acolyte

Raging Bull

Swarmer

Cowpens

Northern Lights

Scorpion

Raging Bull II

Red Light II

Harvest Lights

Sterling

Breakwater

Hastings

Money Worth

Bastogne

Bold Action

Mountain Lion

Cobra Strike

Falcon II

Lion's Pride

Swift Sword

Babil Perimeter

CODA

'In the drawing room the
conversation was still going on.'
—LEO TOLSTOY, 1869

COLLABORATORS

1945

Argentina
Belarus
Brazil
Chile
China
Cuba
Czechoslovakia
Denmark
Dominican Republic
Egypt
El Salvador
France
Haiti
Iran
Lebanon
Luxembourg
New Zealand
Nicaragua
Paraguay
Philippines
Poland
Union of Soviet Socialist Republics
Saudi Arabia
Syrian Arab Republic
Turkey

Ukraine
United Kingdom of Great Britain and
    Northern Ireland
United States of America
Yugoslavia
Greece
India
Peru
Australia
Costa Rica
Liberia
Colombia
Mexico
South Africa
Canada
Ethiopia
Panama
Bolivia
Venezuela
Guatemala
Norway
Netherlands
Honduras
Uruguay
Ecuador
Iraq
Belgium

1946

Afghanistan
Iceland
Sweden
Siam / Thailand

1947

Pakistan
Yemen

1948

Burma / Myanmar

1949

Israel

1950

Indonesia

1955

Albania
Austria
Bulgaria

Cambodia / Khmer Republic / Cambodia /
  Democratic Kampuchea / Cambodia
Finland
Hungary
Ireland
Italy
Jordan
Laos
Libya
Nepal
Portugal
Romania
Spain
Ceylon / Sri Lanka

1956

Morocco
Sudan
Tunisia
Japan

1957

Ghana
Malaya

1958

Guinea

~~Egypt~~

~~Syria~~

United Arab Republic

1960

Dahomey / Benin

Upper Volta / Burkina Faso

Cameroon

Central African Republic / Central African
  Empire / Central African Republic

Chad

Congo

Ivory Coast / Côte d'Ivoire

Cyprus

Democratic Republic of the Congo

Gabon

Malagasy Republic / Madagascar

Niger

Somalia

Togo

Mali

Senegal

Nigeria

1961

Sierra Leone
Mauritania
Mongolia
Tanganyika
Syria

1962

Burundi
Jamaica
Rwanda
Trinidad and Tobago
Algeria
Uganda

1963

Kuwait
Kenya
~~Malaya~~
Malaysia
Zanzibar

1964

Malawi
Malta

Zambia
~~Tanganyika~~
~~Zanzibar~~
Tanzania

1965

Gambia
Maldive Islands / Maldives
Singapore
~~Indonesia~~

1966

Indonesia
Guyana
Botswana
Lesotho
Barbados

1967

Southern Yemen

1968

Mauritius
Swaziland
Equatorial Guinea

1970

Fiji

1971

Bahrain
Bhutan
Qatar
Oman
United Arab Emirates
~~United Arab Republic~~
Egypt

1973

Bahamas
Federal Republic of Germany (West Germany)
German Democratic Republic (East Germany)

1974

Bangladesh
Grenada
Guinea-Bissau

1975

Cabo Verde
Mozambique
Sao Tome and Principe
Papua New Guinea
Comoros
Suriname

1976

Seychelles
Angola
Samoa

1977

Djibouti
Vietnam

1978

Solomon Islands
Dominica

1979

Saint Lucia

1980

Zimbabwe
Saint Vincent and the Grenadines

1981

Vanuatu
Belize
Antigua and Barbuda

1983

Saint Christopher and Nevis / Saint Kitts and
Nevis

1984

Brunei Darussalam

1990

Namibia
Liechtenstein
~~Federal Republic of Germany (West Germany)~~
~~German Democratic Republic (East Germany)~~
Germany
~~Southern Yemen~~

1991

Democratic People's Republic of Korea (North
    Korea)
Estonia
Latvia
Lithuania
Marshall Islands
Micronesia
Republic of Korea (South Korea)
~~Union of Soviet Socialist Republics~~
Russian Federation

1992

Armenia
Azerbaijan
Kazakhstan
Kyrgyzstan
Republic of Moldova
San Marino
Tajikistan
Turkmenistan
Uzbekistan
~~Yugoslavia~~
Bosnia and Herzegovina
Croatia
Slovenia

Georgia

~~Czechoslovakia~~

1993

Czech Republic
Slovakia
Macedonia
Eritrea
Monaco
Andorra

1994

Palau

1999

Kiribati
Nauru
Tonga

2000

Tuvalu
Federal Republic of Yugoslavia / Serbia and
Montenegro

2002

Switzerland
Timor-Leste

2006

Montenegro

ACKNOWLEDGEMENTS

Excerpts of this piece were published in *Harper's Magazine, Geist Magazine, This Magazine* and *Best American Experimental Writing* 2016. The manuscript was also a finalist for the 2014 Les Figues Press Book Prize. Thank you to those publications and their editors.

Operations was exhibited at the Cross Gallery in Taipei, Taiwan, and at Palazzolo Acreide's City Hall. Thank you to those curators.

Several books were helpful while writing the introduction. I'm particularly indebted to Walter Lippmann's *Public Opinion*, Edward Bernays' *Propaganda*, Gregory Nagy's *The Ancient Greek Heroes*, and Gareth Evans' *The Responsibility to Protect: Ending Mass Atrocity Crimes Once and For All*. The Winston Churchill quote is from a memo he wrote on August 8, 1943. The epigraph to the Coda is from Louise and Aylmer Maude's translation of *War and Peace*.

Thank you to the artist residencies that provided the dedicated working time needed to complete this piece. The Taipei Artist Village, and in particular Ching Ching Yang and I-Hua Lee, for the warm welcome and support in Taiwan, and to Stephen Bain and Angelica Nierras for their insights.

Thanks to the Akrai Fellowship, to Claudia Cannizzaro and Turi Scalora in Sicily, and to Monique

Truong and Claudio Beorchia for their spirit.

And for the month in the Okanagan Valley during the Kalamalka Residency, thanks to kevin mcpherson eckhoff, Susan Brandoli, Kalamalka Press and the Caetani House.

At different stages Nina Leo, Jeremy Keehn, Jeff Parker, Carolyn Smart, Charles Bernstein, Hoa Nguyen, Cassidy McFadzean and Karen Solie offered helpful feedback.

Gracious acknowledgement to the Ontario Arts Council for their support, and to the Canada Council for the Arts for their support via Travel Grants.

Rosângela Rennó generously permitted use of her art. Thanks to her and her staff.

And to Jay and Hazel Millar at BookThug, who have been wonderful throughout the process.

Special thanks to Alessandro Porco for the advice, editorial insights, and the ongoing parrhesia.

MOEZ SURANI has travelled, studied, and worked in countries around the world. His writing has been featured in numerous publications, including the *Best Canadian Poetry* (2013 and 2014), *Best American Experimental Writing 2016*, *The Walrus*, *The Globe and Mail*, *Harper's Magazine*, and *PRISM International*. His first poetry collection, *Reticent Bodies*, was published in 2009. In that same year, he won a Chalmers Arts Fellowship, and later attended artists' residencies in Italy, Finland, Latvia, Switzerland, Taiwan, and Canada. His second poetry collection, *Floating Life*, was published in 2012. ةيلمع *Operación Opération Operation* 行动 *Операция*, Surani's third book, was a finalist for 2014 Les Figues Press Book Prize.

COLOPHON

Manufactured as the First Edition of
عمل *Operación Opération Operation* 行动 *Операция*
in the fall of 2016 by BookThug.

Distributed in Canada by the Literary Press Group:
www.lpg.ca
Distributed in the US by Small Press Distribution:
www.spdbooks.org
Shop online at www.bookthug.ca

BOOK
PRODUCTION
WAR ECONOMY
STANDARD

Edited for the press by Alessandro Porco
Type + design by Jay MillAr
Copy edited by Ruth Zuchter